POEMS

ACROSS THE

PAVEMENT

LUIS J. RODRIGUEZ

Tia Chucha Press
Chicago

Acknowledgments

Some of the poems have appeared in the following publications (sometimes in versions different than those collected here): *Scars: American Poetry In the Face of Violence,* edited by Cynthia Dubin Edelberg; *Distinct Voices: A Multicultural Anthology for English as a Second Language Writers,* edited by Jose A. Carmona; *Cool Salsa: Bilingual Poems on Growing Up Latino in the United States,* edited by Lori M. Carlson; *Espacios: Cultura Y Sociedad* (Spanish & English); *Slam Poetry: Heftige Dichtung Aus Amerika* (German translation); *After Aztlan: Latino Writers in the '90s,* edited by Ray Gonzalez; *Crossroads Magazine; Witness Magazine; Americas Review; River Styx; Obras: A Publication of the Beyond Baroque Foundation; Contact II; Left Curve; Poetry East; Compages; Tribuno del Pueblo; Bulletin of El Centro de Estudios Puertorriquenos of Hunters College, New York City; San Fernando Poetry Journal; Poetry Connection: Dial-A-Poem Chicago.*

Thanks to Deborah Pintonelli, Reginald Gibbons, Jack Hirschman, Richard Bray, Lew Rosenbaum, Carlos Cumpian, Michael Warr, Gregorio Gomez and the "Weeds" and "Gallery Cabaret" poets. Also thanks to members of the Los Angeles Latino Writers Association, Theater Workers Project of the United Steelworkers Local 1845 and the Latino Chicago Theater Company, who at one time or another helped bring some of my works to life.

And a special thanks to my wife, Maria Trinidad Rodriguez, for her patience and support.

This book won a 1989 Poetry Center Book Award, San Francisco State University. Thanks to all the people at The Poetry Center and judge, Jimmy Santiago Baca.

Printed in the United States of America.
Second Printing, 1991. Third Printing, 1993. Fourth Printing, 1996.

ISBN 0-9624287-0-1
Library of Congress Catalog Card Number 90-119897

Book design: Jane Brunette
Cover art: Detail from "The Window" by Gamaliel Ramírez

PUBLISHED BY:
TIA CHUCHA PRESS
A Project of the Guild Complex
PO Box 476969
Chicago, IL 60647

DISTRIBUTED BY:
NORTHWESTERN UNIVERSITY PRESS
Chicago Distribution Center
11030 S. Langley
Chicago, IL 60628

This project was partially supported by grants from the City of Chicago Department of Cultural Affairs, Office of Fine Arts, the Illinois Arts Council and the National Endowment for the Arts.

To
Ramiro Daniel,
Andrea Victoria
and
Rubén   Joaquín

Contents

Running to America

*T*hey are night shadows
  violating borders;
fingers curled through chain-link fences,
hiding from infra-red eyes,
dodging 30-30 bullets.
They leave familiar smells,
warmth and sounds
as ancient
as the trampled stones.

Running to America.

There is a woman
in her finest
border-crossing wear:
A purple blouse from
an older sister, a pair of worn
shoes from a church bazaar.
A tattered coat
from a former lover.

There is a child
dressed in black.
Fear sparkling from
dark Indian eyes;
clinging to
a beheaded Barbie doll.

*For Alfonso and
María Estela;
immigrants.*

And the men,
some hardened, quiet.
Others young and loud.
You see something like this
in prisons.

1

Soon they will cross
on their bellies; kissing
black earth.

Running to America.

Strange voices
whisper behind garbage cans,
beneath freeway passes,
next to broken bottles.
The spatter of words,
textured and multi-colored,
invoke demons.

They must run to America.

Their skin,
color of earth,
is a brand
for all the great ranchers,
for the killing floors
on Soto Street,
and as slaughter
for the garment row.
Still they come.
A hungry people
have no country.

Their tears
are the grease
of the bobbing machines
that rip into cloth
that make clothes
that keep you warm.

They have endured
the sun's stranglehold,
el cortito,

foundry heats
and dark caves
of mines
hungry for men.

Still they come,
wandering bravely
through the thickness
of this strange land's
maddening ambivalence.

Their cries are singed
with fires of hope.
Their babies are born
with a lion
in their hearts.
Who can confine them?
Who can tell them
which lines never to cross?

For the green rivers,
for their looted gold,
escaping the blood of a land
that threatens to drown them,

they have come,
running to America.

I Hear a Saxophone

I hear a saxophone
   crying out tunes
in deep colors;
of blues
of reds
of yellows.

Every street voice,
every longing child,
every mother's song
blends through
this brass throat,

stirring dust,
coalescing with
a cat's perverted wail,
tires screeching,
a Spanish curse,
floating through thin walls.

I hear a saxophone,
plucking notes
from heart beats;
a cacophony of crippled cries.

*Sweet music
came in through the
side window of a
three-story flat.
The poem came next.*

echoes . . .
echoes . . .
echoes . . .
pounding
into a purified exchange
between woodwind
and soul.

String Bean

1.
Come to this shrine,
a living room altar;
a raised place
for statues of *santos,*
surrounded by candles,
adorned with rosary beads and flowers.

Come. Touch the icons
of *La Virgen de Guadalupe,*
Niño Jesus and a doll-like figure
of *San Judas,*
each with outstretched hands
and small flowing robes.

Come hear *mi amá's* encantations;
lighting candles over expressionless faces,
over painted blood
on a bust of a blue-eyed Jesus.

Mi amá—always on her knees,
either praying or scrubbing floors.

*Thanks to
Reynalda Palacios.*

2.
Next to *La Virgen,* in a place of near sainthood,
stood a portrait of my Indian grandmother.
Mama prayed to her.

She prayed for food
on the days in between my father's lay-offs.
She prayed for my brother and me,
who played in the hidden spaces
of sewer tunnels and hobo nests

by the railroad tracks.
She prayed we would come home
without blood pouring from some wound.

She prayed for her daughters,
a common prayer for all women.
She prayed they would grow up unviolated
in spirit, body and mind.
She prayed for the kind of strength
that had taken Mama through a drunken father,
nightly beatings and seeing her mother
dragged by the hair.

3.
Sundays in the *barrio*,
people emerged from lop-sided and peeling
wood-frame homes in the finest attire.
They converged on the church.
Even the craziest dudes
had *La Virgen*
tattooed on their backs.
Every time somebody cruised by the church,
they crossed themselves.

4.
Children piled into Sunday school classes.
Nuns in black with wrinkled faces
punished some for speaking out,
for laughing behind their backs or being late.
There are bottle caps where children knelt
for what seemed hours.

One time a nun asked a little girl,
"Who is God?"
The girl got up from her seat,
nervous, fearful.
Finally, after a slow start, she replied,
"God ees a string bean."
The class went into an uproar.
The nun gasped in horror.

She grabbed a ruler from her desk,
rushed up to the trembling girl
and smacked the inside of the girl's hand.
It took a while before she had realized
the girl had meant to say,
"God is a supreme being."

Rosalie Has Candles

Rosalie has candles in a circle around her bed.
One night as I lay on a couch
in a tequila stupor,
she takes off my shoes and trousers,
pulls a cover over me and snips
two inches of hair from my head.
She places the hair in a glass
near the candles. I don't know why.
I don't know why she searches for me.
I don't know how she finds me in the bars.
I don't know why she ridicules the women I like
and uses me to meet men.
Rosalie usually finds solace in a glass
of whiskey. In my face she finds the same thing.
I don't know why. We argue too much.
We feign caring and then hurt each other
with indifference. With others we are tough
and mean. But in the quiet of darkness
we hold each other and caress like kittens.
She says she can only make love to someone
when she is drunk. She says she loves men
but has lesbian friends.
She loves being looked at. I want to hide.
She hates struggle. That's all I do.
She has Gods to pray to. I just curse.
I don't know what she sees in my face,
or hands for that matter. I only know
she needs me like whiskey.

The Monster

*I*t erupted into our lives:
  Two guys in jeans shoved it
through the door—
heaving & grunting & biting lower lips.

A large industrial sewing machine.
We called it "the monster."

It came on a winter's day,
rented out of mother's pay.
Once in the living room
the walls seemed to cave in around it.

Black footsteps to our door
brought heaps of cloth for Mama to sew.
Noises of war burst out of the living room.
Rafters rattled. Floors farted—
the radio going into static
each time the needle ripped into fabric.

Many nights I'd get up from bed,
wander squinty-eyed down a hallway
and peer through a dust-covered blanket
to where Mama and the monster
did nightly battle.

I could see Mama through the yellow haze
of a single light bulb.
She, slouched over the machine.
Her eyes almost closed.
Her hair in disheveled braids;

each stitch binding her life
to scraps of cloth.

"Race" Politics

My brother and I
—shopping for *la jefita*—
decided to get the "good food"
over on the other side
of the tracks.

We dared each other.
Laughed a little.
Thought about it.
Said, what's the big deal.
Thought about that.
Decided we were men,
not boys.
Decided we should go wherever
we damn wanted to.

Oh, my brother—now he was bad.
Tough dude. Afraid of nothing.
I was afraid of him.

So there we go,
climbing over
the iron and wood ties,
over discarded sofas
and bent-up market carts,
over a weed-and-dirt road,
into a place called South Gate
—all white. All American.

We entered the forbidden
narrow line of hate,
imposed,
transposed,

For my brother,
"the Frog."

supposed,
a line of power/powerlessness
full of meaning,
meaning nothing—
those lines that crisscross
the abdomen of this land,
that strangle you
in your days, in your nights.
When you dream.

There we were, two Mexicans,
six and nine—from Watts no less.
Oh, this was plenty reason
to hate us.

Plenty reason to run up behind us.
Five teenagers on bikes.
Plenty reason to knock
the groceries out from our arms—
    a splattering heap of soup
    cans, bread and candy.

Plenty reason to hold me down
on the hot asphalt; melted gum,
    and chips of broken
    beer bottle on my lips
    and cheek.

Plenty reason to get my brother
by the throat, taking turns
    punching him in the face,
    cutting his lower lip,
    punching, him vomiting.
Punching until swollen and dark blue
he slid from their grasp
like a rotten banana from its peeling.

When they had enough, they threw us back,
dirty and lacerated;
back to Watts, its towers shiny
across the orange-red sky.

ll

My brother then forced me
to promise not to tell anybody
how he cried.
He forced me to swear to God,
to Jesus Christ, to our long-dead
Indian Grandmother —
keepers of our meddling souls.

Tombstone Poets

*L*eaning against fractured tombstones,
   we wove poems, Micaela and me;
grabbing strands from sunken lives,
creating an alchemy of words,
interlaced with a needle-induced glow;
     sparking prose out of
     the poverty of unreason.

Ragged memories pushed tongues
into cheap chatter; recalling port wine,
     jail nights—the terror time
     between 2 a.m. and the first light of day
     without lovers.

And the *tecata* look in her smile,
so distant even as she gazed into my eyes,
here beneath an eastside sun.

Precious, precious, precious . . .
the noon-hours at Evergreen cemetery.
Paper lunch bags at our side.

Even now, I hear the humming from her soul.

But heroin took her home from me.
Strings of words suspended in mist,
like broken webs.
Only protruding headstones remain,

mute witnesses to when life glowed afire,
when Micaela and me wove tempestuous silk,
leaning on slabs of chipped stone.

Lucinda

*S*anta Ana winds
    forced my VW bug
to dance across
Interstate 10
as I drove for hours
toward home.

To your door:
Lucinda, of the light hair
and dark eyes.

The VW looked the way I had lived:
Scars of eight auto accidents
and a crumpled license plate,
half falling off.
Each door a different
shade of topaz.
Worn tires encircled
rusted chrome rims.

But it brought me closer to you,
Lucinda of the crystalline smile.

Large tractor-trailer rigs
rumbled by the bug,
waking me often
from slumber at the wheel.

Lucinda, of the old Rocky mountains
and Apache earth,
I cried out your name.

You led me with those eyes

that smiled a different song.
I wanted to live in them.

You led me with desert-night talks,
of old times, other loves,
and the misreading of signals.

You beckoned with the words:
      I love you.
Muttered while drunk
on gin and vermouth
and nodding out
at eastside *cantinas*.

Lucinda of the light hair.
Mother of daughters.
How I sought you.
At street corners,
shit-kicking bars,
and on that wretched highway
from San Berdoo to shaky-town.

Oh, Lucinda,
of the smooth music,
quiet mountain streams,
and breaking of ocean waves.

Of dark dresses,
ruffled and violated.

Of bottles smashed over heads,
knife scars
and stretch marks
you tried so hard to hide.

How I sought you.

Palmas

Palmas swayed
　on a rickety porch
near an old eaten-up tree
and plucked at a six-string:
The guitar man
of the 'hood.

Fluid fingers
moved across the neck
like a warm wind
across one's brow.

Each chord
filled with pain,
glory and boozed-up nights.

Every note sweating.

On Saturdays,
Palmas jammed with local dudes.
They played in his honor
on the nights
he didn't show up.

The guitar man:
So sick. So tired.
But, man, he played so sweet.

I often wondered
what gave Palmas his magic.
Blues bands wanted him.
Norteño bands wanted him.
Jazz musicians

called out his name
from the bandstand.

He played Wes Montgomery
as if the dude
were living inside his head.

He played
crisp *corridos* and *Jarocho* blues
and seemed to make Jeff Beck
float through
the living room window.

Yet, he didn't venture
too far beyond his rickety porch.

Sometimes
he sat alone in his room,
the guitar
on a corner
of an unmade bed.

The last I heard,
he played only
when the heroin in his body
gave him a booking.

With Stone Hands and Fire Eyes

*I*nvestors in brain damage,
anemic men in grey suits
placidly await your sacrifice
on the altar of profits.

Brown
Mexica priests,
with stone hands
and fire eyes,
stand solid
like forged iron.

Black
Mandingo warriors
hungry cobras
in factory furnaces
strike first.
Survivors.

Black and brown.
You pursue.
Stalk.
Throwing blows
like gun-fire,
conditioned
under sweaty lights
in archaic gyms.
Prepared
for the last dance.

You think Ali
You think Duran
You think Sugar Ray,

heeding
the longing for heroes.

Voices, cutting through smoky
arenas like blunt knives
clamoring for a violent poetry
written in blood.

No Work Today

*T*he sign on the door said:
"No Work Today."

I walked in anyway.
I'd be damned if I was going
to spend $2 on bus fare,
an hour on the freeway,
and face the funny looks of suburbanites
only to find there's no work.
I'd be damned.

"Give me an application."

"Sorry buddy, no jobs."

"Well, give me an application anyway."

"Hey, save yourself the trouble . . .
there ain't no work today,
there was no work yesterday,
and who knows what tomorrow
is going to bring?"

"Listen, I took two buses,
walked five blocks and killed
a good part of the morning
getting here. The least I should get
is an application."

"I'm telling you, it would be a
waste of time.
There's no work. Read my lips:
N-O-W-O-R-K."

I mean, cars get killed everyday.
I understood this pain.
And every time he swung down on the metal,
I felt the blue heat swim up his veins.
I sensed the seething eye staring from his chest,
the gleam of sweat on his neck,
the anger of a thousand sneers—
the storm of bright lights
into the abyss of an eyeball.
Lonely? Out of work? Out of time?
I knew this pain. I wanted to be there—
to yell out with him,
to squeeze out the violence
that gnawed at his throat.
I wanted to be the sledge hammer,
to be the crush of steel on glass,
to be this angry young man;
a woman at my side.

Alabama

Alabama—
seared mouths speak
smothered by timbers of cedar,
blaring out the cries
of a pained land.

Alabama is rained-soaked shacks
and children born into seclusion
behind walls of betrayed promises.

Alabama is air like humid hands
grabbing throats and pushing bodies
into wet earth to harvest again.

From darkened skies come storm clouds
with deadly showers
chipping away
the broken gravestones
of the living dead,
now come to life;
to the slave auction blocks,
now innocent kiosks in the grass;
to the obelisk monument
for Nathan Bedford Forest—the first Klansman,
now painted over with
"Free the Black Belt."

*During black
empowerment
elections in the
Alabama Black Belt,
I came face to face
with America.*

Nurtured by rays of sun
and luminous dew drops
power here is sought
as if it is water
to thirsty lips.

Alabama is green
It is red.
It is black.

Beautiful, foliage green,
spilling blood red,
and life-giving earth black.

Alabama is a burial ground,
an enslaved country,
that keeps calling us back.

Juchitán

I
1.
n the *zócalo*, the banter
of black birds rises
as the afternoon rolls in
and people come to gather.

This is a place
so removed from home—and so close.
Of tropical scents,
brightly-colored *huipiles*
and an ancient language
whispered by children at play,
women relating the news
and drunks brawling over obscure points.

An odor of beef heads—eyes bulging—
cooking in open *taco* stands
satiates the humid air.
Tehuanas, wide Indian women
with hearty laughs and round faces,
prepare fish and *iguanas*
for the marketplace.

I once covered Anti-government protests in this Oaxacan coastal town. Mexican troops had already landed.

I slice a path
through the dampness,
the children's laughter
and singing of black birds

2.
White metal benches
fill with young lovers,
the elderly
and sleepy-eyed.

Teenagers scamper by in T-shirts that say:
Juchitán: Capital del Mundo—
Juchitán: Capital of the World.

Every scraped eye,
every hungry cry,
finds shape in *Juchitán.*
Every oppressor's fear,
every liberator's spear,
is alive in *Juchitán.*

Harried merchants call to one another.
A young mother pokes out a brown breast.
Across the street, government troops
calmly cradle machine guns.

3.
A pile of rocks
lie near a large bell
on top of the municipal palace.
From here, the movement
of troops is studied.
At signs of attack
the bell is to be tolled—
to call out *'tecos*
from farms, homes and the marketplace.
They have no weapons.
Save sticks. Save rocks.

The voting is today.
Government supporters have beaten
two foreign journalists, accused of truth.
Truckloads of paid voters
come in shifts from nearby towns.
The *'tecos* march on muddy paths,
past thatched-roofed huts,
in protest.
Late at night, troops move closer.
I'm stuck on the *palacio's* third floor.
Next to the bell.

Journalists are told to leave.
I pick up a rock.

4.
"They're going to kill you,"
a taxi driver informs me.
It's 4 a.m.
All night long, the government ruling party
held feasts. Armed guards
protected their revelry.
The government has stolen the elections.
Thousands of *'tecos*
assemble at the *palacio* to hear
their defeated representatives,
in the music of the *Zapoteca* tongue,
hold high their centuries-old
war of liberation.

"I know," I tell the taxi driver,
"but take me to the bus station anyway."
It's not safe for sympathetic *"gringos"*
(even if brown) to stay around.
I carry the *Juchitécos'* struggle
in a journal and in film.

The taxi driver looks at me hard
—then laughs.
"You must be crazier than I am,"
and takes my bag. I clinch the camera.
A lone pig wobbles along a dirt road.

Overtown 1984

Overtown—you are the last shred of America
   left in America.
You are the last ones to remain mute
   in the face of destruction.
You are the long evening descended
   into daybreak.
From the sockets of burning skulls
   come screams of retribution,
For our sons, for our daughters,
      for fathers forced into not being fathers,
      for mothers who only see the world
      through the tunnel of a child's long wail.

When you awoke again in flames,
   you carried me with you;
You, a face of fire, sweat across furrowed
   foreheads.
You, the bones of a dark time,
   of a stumbling down dilapidated steps.
It seemed an act of desperation, you alone
   against the Miami skies.

*I worked in Miami
once. At that time a
jury had acquitted a
policeman for killing
a young Overtown
man. An uprising
followed.*

Alone in the shadow of palm trees.
Alone against the blackened batons
      of police power.
Alone against the newspapers & TV stations &
      suited officials at bus stops &
      politicians in marbled corridors
      who dared to call you "criminals."
Newspapers carried pictures of Overtown
      residents in paddy wagons, looking tired,
      forlorned.

Alone? Not really. Your long night took me in.

I watched the burning from outside my hotel
      room following the acquittal of a police
      officer who killed an unarmed
      Overtown boy.
Walking toward you, I was met by helmeted
      officers. By whirling lights and road blocks.
      I kept coming.
Near some apartments a boy started a fire.
Its flames were the brothers of Watts, Detroit,
      the Hough and Harlem.
Near a place of murder along a cement path,
      life came to life.
Under the street lamps, under freeway passes
      and green palms, the darkness became
      glowy and red.
The voices of children rose up
      like thunderous sonatas.

Tomatoes

When you bite
deep to the core
of a ripe, juicy tomato,
sing a psalm
for Margarito Lupercio.

Praise the 17-year existence
of an immigrant tomato picker.

But don't bother to look
for his fingerprints
on the thin tomato skins.

They are implanted
on the banks
of the Delta Mendota Canal,
imbedded on soft soil
where desperate fingers
grasped and pulled,
reaching out
to silent shadows on shore
as deadly jaws
of rushing water
pulled him to its belly.

*The poem draws
from an account
that appeared in a
California Central
Valley newspaper.*

Margarito had jumped in,
so he could keep working;
to escape,
    miserly taunts,
    stares of disdain;
    indignities of alienhood
to escape,

Border Patrol officers tearing across
a tomato field like cowboys,
to escape,
the iron bars of desert cells
and hunger's dried-up face.

A brother of the fields
heard Margarito's cries
as the Migra officers watched
and did nothing.

He tied together torn sheets,
shirts, loose rope—
anything he could find,
pleading for help
in the anxious tones
that overcome language barriers.

Officers, in your name,
watched
and did nothing.

Workers later found Margarito's body
wedged in the entrails
of a sluice gate.
They delivered it to town,
tomato capital of the world,
awakened now, suddenly,
to the tyranny of indifference.

Piece by Piece

*P*iece by piece
    They tear at you:
Peeling away layers of being,
Lying about who you are,
Speaking for your dreams.

In the squalor of their eyes
You are an outlaw.
Dressing you in a jacket of lies
—tailor made in steel—
You fit their perfect picture.

Take it off!
Make your own mantle.
Question the interrogators.
Eyeball the death in their gaze.
Say you won't succumb.
Say you won't believe them
When they rename you.
Say you won't accept their codes,
Their colors, their putrid morals.

Here you have a way.
Here you can sing victory.
Here you are not a conquered race
Perpetual victim—
The sullen face in a thunderstorm.

Hands/mind, they are carving out
A sanctuary.
Use these weapons against them.
Use your given gifts—
They are not stone.

Walk Late Chicago

Walk late, this cold town.
Walk late and see those
who have nothing to do but walk.
Who have to walk to stay alive.
Who walk the pot-holed, scarred streets
to a second's safety,
of alleys littered with rat carcasses,
of abandoned buildings
and heaps of cardboard and cloth.

Walk late in zero weather,
zero less than a number,
less than the loneliest day.
This is zero less than a heartbeat.
The zero of death. The stillness
of no tomorrows. A deep, sickening,
empty zero of a late night walk
in this cold town.

On a damp corner, snow is piled
black and white to the edge
of a soot-and-red brick building.
Here is the only hope still burning
this late night, of this late walk.

*From a night at a
homeless shelter.*

Come in, brother. Keep warm, brother.
What's your name, brother?
You been here before?
You're in luck.
One place still there for you.
You got a name? Hey it's okay.
There's room. What's your name?

34

I had a name once.
It meant something . . . once.
But now what's a name.
What's a smile, a good laugh,
when all there is zero;
less than the darkest shadow
of the darkest corner
I've ever laid in.

Okay, brother. Follow me, brother.
It's okay. I walk slow, tired,
stepping over mattresses
stepping over humanity,
crowded into a converted warehouse,
filled with men—
women and children in another room.

I enter a dark cavern.
On the ceiling are rows of pipes
and tracks for what used
to hold overhead cranes.
On the ground are more bodies,
some on beds, most on the floor.
Somebody tells me to pull a mattress
from a pile. Tells me
to walk over to a corner
of this dark warehouse.

      Boils on flesh. Coughing,
deep, bloody coughs. Whispering voices.
Hollering. They say I'm mad,
but this is madness.

On a crowded corner,
I throw the mattress on a small
empty spot near a red-faced,
lice-infested man coughing up TB.
I take off my shoes,
lay them next to a wall,
look up into a statue of Jesus

with outstretched hands
and imploring eyes of painted plaster.

Sleep. Bed bugs play havoc on skin.
Sleep. Sleep of tension;
sleep like no other sweet sleep.
Sleep of zero.

Early—6 a.m.—darkness still bathing
the warehouse. Voices break up
the glory of sleep.
Get up, everybody, get up. Time to go.
Slowly pick up what ever belongs to me.
Possessions. Don't laugh.
Shoes still there
wrapped up in a beanie cap.
Praise to shoes!

I make my way into
a loading dock area, crowded now.
Standing around, I stare at faces,
talk about the latest Cub's game . . .
the Pope's last visit.

People in front pass out
coffee and a granola bar.
Women can be heard now,
a couple of children standing near.

Soon the dock's metal doors creak open.
Vans with daily newspapers wait outside,
ready to take those who can
hawk them on street corners
and entrances to expressways.

While some pile into the vans,
others walk on to find a warm place
'til the day shelters open—hours still.
I feel the sting as the wet cold
slaps across my face.

Holding on to a near-empty
cup of coffee, I enter
a heartless dawn.

The Calling

*T*he calling came to me
   while I languished
in my room; while I
whittled away my youth
in jail cells
and damp *barrio* fields.

It brought me to life,
out of captivity,
in a street-scarred
and tattooed place
I called body.

Until then I waited silently,
a deafening clamor in my head,
but voiceless to all around me;
hidden from America's eyes,
A brown boy without a name,

I would sing into a solitary
   tape recorder,
music never to be heard.
I would write my thoughts
in scrambled English;
I would take photos in my mind—
   plan out new parks;
   bushy green, concrete free.
   New places to play
   and think.

Waiting.
Then it came.
The calling.

*First written
at the age of 16.*

It brought me out of my room.
It forced me to escape
night captors
in street prisons.

It called me to war;
to be writer,
to be scientist
and march with the soldiers
        of change.

It called me from the shadows,
out of the wreckage,
of my *barrio*—from among those
who did not exist.

I waited all of 16 years
for this time.

Somehow, unexpected,
I was called.

About the Author

Luis J. Rodriguez is the award-winning author of *Always Running: La Vida Loca, Gang Days in L.A.,* for which he received the 1993 Carl Sandburg Prize for Nonfiction and the 1994 Chicago Sun-Times First Prose Book Award. His two books of poetry—*Poems Across the Pavement* and *The Concrete River*—have won the Poetry Center Book Award from San Francisco State University and the PEN West/Josephine Miles Award for Literary Excellence. In 1992, he received a prestigious Lannan Fellowship in Poetry.

His poetry, essays, reviews and stories have appeared in the *Los Angeles Times, The Nation, U.S. News & World Report, The Utne Reader, Philadelphia Inquirer Magazine, Hungry Mind Review, Poets & Writers* and *The Chicago Reporter,* among others. Luis is also founder/publisher of Tia Chucha Press, a poetry press based in Chicago and the publishing wing of the Guild Complex.

Luis has traveled extensively across the country lecturing, reading and conducting workshops in prisons, schools, universities, homeless shelters, migrant camps, community centers, juvenile facilities and bookstores. He has also performed in Montreal, Toronto, Paris, London, Rome, Amsterdam and across Germany and Austria. His journalism travels have also taken him to Mexico, Central America and Puerto Rico.

Born in El Paso, Texas, Luis was raised in Los Angeles and currently lives in Chicago. He has four children and two grandchildren.